What is green and stays outside?

Paddy O'Furniture

What did the leprechaun learn in school?

The elf-abet!

Why are potatoes good detectives?

Because they keep their eyes peeled.

How can you tell
if an Irishman
is having
a good time?

He's Dublin over
with laughter.

What's the
best month
for a parade?

March!

Knock Knock.
Who's there?
Irish.
Irish who?
Irish you a happy
St. Patrick's Day!

Published by The Millbrook Press, Inc.
2 Old New Milford Road
Brookfield, CT 06804
www.millbrookpress.com

Library of Congress Cataloging-in-Publication Data

Roop, Peter.
Let's celebrate St. Patrick's Day/by Peter and Connie Roop ;
illustrated by Gwen Connelly.
p. cm.
Summary: Examines the history, customs, and folklore of
St. Patrick'sDay. Includes a craft, a recipe, and jokes and riddles.
ISBN 0-7613-2505-0 (lib. bdg.)
ISBN 0-7613-7182-1 (pbk.)
1. Saint Patrick's Day—Juvenile literature. (1. Saint Patrick's Day.
2. Holidays.)  I. Roop, Connie.  II. Connelly, Gwen, ill.  III. Title.
GT4995.P3    R65    2003
394.262—dc21  2002006485

# Let's Celebrate
# St. Patrick's Day

By Peter and Connie Roop

Illustrated by Gwen Connelly

The Millbrook Press
Brookfield, Connecticut

For Charlie and Kakie–
Keep Those Irish Eyes Smiling!

You dress in a green shirt and green pants. Your classroom is decorated with green shamrocks, green balloons, and green leprechauns. Your teacher greets everyone saying, "Top o' the morning, class!" What day is it?

# St. Patrick's Day!

# Why do we celebrate St. Patrick's Day?

St. Patrick's Day is celebrated on March 17. It is a day to honor Saint Patrick, who died on March 17 about 1,500 years ago. All over America there are parades, parties, and church services to remember him. Why? Because he was a well-loved man who helped spread Christianity through Ireland.

# Who was Saint Patrick?

Saint Patrick was born in Britain around the year A.D. 385. His name was Maewyn Succat. His family was Roman, and they were nobles. Many Romans lived in Britain long ago. Patrick's father owned farms and had servants. Patrick probably did not have to work in the fields or in the house as he grew up.

One day, when Patrick was sixteen, pirates from Ireland raided Britain. Patrick was captured and taken to Ireland. There he was sold as a slave to an Irish chief named Miliuc.

Miliuc sent Patrick to take care of his sheep. Shepherds spent many lonely months caring for their flocks in pastures far from town. For six years Patrick spent a lot of time thinking and praying. One night Patrick had a dream in which an angel told him to run away. He walked 200 miles (320 kilometers) to the coast, where there was a ship about to sail. Patrick boarded that ship and his life was changed forever.

# How did Patrick become a Saint?

The ship took Patrick to France where he decided to become a priest. He would devote his life to God. He studied in France and spent some time in a monastery there. When he became a priest he took the name *Patrick*. Then he went to Rome, where the pope made him a bishop of the Catholic Church. The pope asked Patrick to go back to Ireland. He wanted Patrick to tell the Irish people about Christianity.

In Ireland, Patrick went to see the high king of Tara. After talking with Patrick, the king chose to accept Patrick's religion. Patrick spent the rest of his life preaching in Ireland. Many people joined the Catholic Church, and many churches were built.

When Patrick died, the Irish people were very sad. For twelve days and nights people came to mourn him. One story says that the sun shone all twelve days. Patrick was made a saint, and his life and works have been remembered ever since.

Another name for St. Patrick's Day is St. Paddy's Day. *Paddy* is a nickname for *Patrick*.

People in Ireland speak two languages: English and Gaelic, which is an old Irish language.

*Erin Go Braugh!* means "Ireland forever!"

Every year millions of shamrocks from Ireland are shipped to America.

There are more Irish signers of the Declaration of Independence than from any other country.

# What stories do people tell about Saint Patrick?

Saint Patrick was so popular during his life that, when he died, people added a little here and there to make him sound even better in the stories they told their children and grandchildren. One story has to do with snakes. There are no snakes in Ireland. People say it is because Saint Patrick drove them into the sea.

Another story says that Saint Patrick made the ground in Ireland poisonous to snakes. If they touch it, they will die. The truth is that there never were snakes in Ireland. But the story of this "good deed" by Saint Patrick has now become a popular legend.

# Why do we celebrate St. Patrick's Day in America?

Many years after Patrick died, the English ruled Ireland. They made many laws that were unfair. Irish children could not go to school. Irish people could not own land. Many Irish were so poor that they had little to eat. Potatoes grew well in Ireland, and many families ate them for breakfast, lunch, and dinner.

One year a terrible disease attacked the potatoes. They turned black in the soil. The plants died. No potatoes meant nothing to eat. Thousands of people died. There was not enough food for families to stay together.

But in America there was food. And there were jobs. Many Irish families moved to America in the mid-1800s. So many Irish came to America that there are more people in America with Irish relatives than there are in Ireland! With them the Irish brought their hero, Saint Patrick. The Irish had celebrated St. Patrick's Day in Ireland. When they came to America they brought that tradition with them.

# How do the Irish celebrate St. Patrick's Day in Ireland?

In Ireland, St. Patrick's Day is a national holiday. Children have the day off from school. No mail is delivered. Banks are closed, too.

Many Irish people go to church on St. Patrick's Day. It is also a time for family. Many families have special meals. They might eat Irish soda bread, Irish stew, or colcannon, which is made with potatoes, cabbage, and onions. Friends might gather at the neighborhood pub to celebrate together.

In 1995 the Irish government started the St. Patrick's Day Festival. The first festival was held in 1996 in Dublin. They have a big parade. There is music and dancing, food, crafts, and fireworks. The celebration lasts for four days. It is the largest annual celebration in Ireland.

# How do we celebrate St. Patrick's Day in America?

St. Patrick's Day is not a national holiday in America. But Americans everywhere celebrate the day. There is a saying that on St. Patrick's Day, "Everyone is Irish!"

There are a lot of parades in America on St. Patrick's Day. The biggest is in New York City. Bands march and play Irish songs. People carry Irish flags and banners. There are decorated floats. The parade passes in front of St. Patrick's Cathedral. Sometimes it lasts as long as six hours! A traditional meal in America on St. Patrick's day is corned beef and cabbage.

# Fascinating Facts

The Chicago River is dyed green on St. Patrick's Day.

The first St. Patrick's Day parade in America was in Boston, in 1737.

In 1780, General George Washington gave his troops the day off on March 17. Many of his soldiers were Irish.

If you don't wear green on St. Patrick's Day, people can pinch you!

There is a Shamrock, Texas. A monument there has an actual piece of the Blarney Stone.

# Why is everything green on St. Patrick's Day?

Ireland is often called the Emerald Isle. An emerald is a beautiful green jewel.

Ireland gets a lot of rain. Grass, shamrocks, and trees grow very well all year round. The Irish countryside is a deep, lush green. Some people say there is no other green like Irish emerald green.

Ireland uses the color green in its flag. Its flag used to be green with a yellow harp in the center. In the early 1900s, Ireland changed it to three stripes of green, white, and orange. Green stands for the Irish people. Orange stands for the English, who ruled Ireland for so long. The white stripe in the middle stands for peace between the two.

# Why is the three-leaf clover a symbol of St. Patrick's Day?

That three-leaf clover is called a shamrock. The word comes from the old Irish word *seamrog*, which means "little clover."

Legend says that Saint Patrick used the shamrock to explain Christianity. He said that one leaf stands for God. The second leaf stands for Jesus. The third leaf stands for the Holy Ghost.

The shamrock became a popular Irish symbol. Irish soldiers began wearing shamrocks on their uniforms to show how proud they were to be Irish. Once when the English queen Victoria was angry at her Irish soldiers, she ordered them not to wear shamrocks on their uniforms. The Irish people were very angry that the queen banned the shamrock. This made the shamrock even more popular as a symbol of Ireland.

# What's a Leprechaun?

In Irish folklore, a leprechaun is a small old elf who stands about 2 feet (60 centimeters) tall. He will almost always be alone, perhaps because he is almost always very bad-tempered.

Irish folklore has lots of fairies in it, and when you hear enough of the stories you will know that fairies are always dancing. The leprechauns' job is to make and mend the fairies' shoes. For this, leprechauns are paid with gold pieces.

Leprechauns store their gold in great big pots that are sometimes found where the rainbow ends.

To catch a leprechaun you must listen for the *tap-tap-tap* of his tiny hammer. To catch him, you must tell him you will hurt him. Then he must show you his pot of gold. Beware! If you take your eyes off of the leprechaun, even to blink, he will disappear.

Why did the leprechaun jump up and down on his potatoes?

*He wanted mashed potatoes for dinner!*

Shenanigans are tricks played by leprechauns.

What did the harp say to the mean leprechaun?

*Stop picking on me!*

What kind of music do leprechauns like?

*Sham Rock!*

# What is the Blarney stone?

Kissing the Blarney stone is something tourists do when they visit Ireland. It is a stone set in a wall in Blarney Castle. Why would people kiss it? Legend says that this stone has a magic spell on it.

According to the story, an old woman put a spell on the stone to thank the king of the castle for rescuing her. All the king had to do was kiss the stone and he would be able to charm people into doing exactly what he wanted. This was a great gift! The word *blarney* has come to mean nonsense or empty flattery.

There is a town in Ireland called Limerick. That is also the name of a silly, five-line poem. To write a limerick, make the last word in the first, second, and fifth lines rhyme, and the last word in the third and fourth lines rhyme. Here's one for you:

There once was a wee leprechaun named Ted
Who did not want to get out of bed.
"My clothes are all green,
That's all I have seen,
Just once can't I wear something red?"

The most famous poet who wrote limericks was Edward Lear.
Here are some of his limericks:

There was an Old Man of Kilkenny,
Who never had more than a penny;
He spent all that money,
In onions and honey,
That wayward Old Man of Kilkenny.

There was an Old Man with a beard,
Who said, "It is just as I feared!
Two Owls and a Hen,
Four Larks and a Wren,
Have all built their nests in my beard!"

# Grow Your Own Potatoes

Potatoes are an important food in Ireland.
These beautiful plants are easy to grow.

## Materials:

Jar
Water
Toothpicks
Potato (the older the better!)

Fill a jar with water.
Put three toothpicks around your potato.
Balance your potato on top of the jar so that about half the potato is
in the water.
Watch your potato sprout roots and green shoots.

**GHEAUGHTEIGHPTOUGH** spells POTATO! How? In the Irish language
of Gaelic, here is how these letter combinations sound:

GH is P, as in *hiccough*        EIGH is A, as in *eight*
EAU is O, as in *beau*           PT is T, as in *pteradactyl*
GHT is T, as in *night*          OUGH is O, as in *though*

## POTATO!

# Ideas for a green
# St. Patrick's Day Feast

## Bake a Shamrock Cake!

### Materials:
Cake mix for a layer cake
Heart-shaped cake pans
7 sandwich cookies
White frosting
Green food coloring

Prepare the cake mix according to the directions.
Divide the cake batter into three equal parts.
Bake three heart-shaped cakes. Get help when working around a hot
  oven. If you have only one heart-shaped pan, wait until one layer is
  baked and then reuse the pan.
Arrange your cakes and cookies as shown.
Put a few drops of green food coloring in the frosting container and stir.
Frost all with green frosting.

Then add:

limeade,
green Jell-o squares,
kiwi fruit,
celery,
green peppers, and
mint ice cream.

Who is a famous
Irish magician?

**Saint Pat-TRICK**

What is raised in
Ireland during the
rainy season?

**Umbrellas**

Who is a famous
Irish purple
dinosaur?

**Blarney**

When is an
Irish potato not
an Irish potato?

When it's a
FRENCH fry!

How are tuna fish
and an Irish harp
different?

You can't
tune a fish.

Where would you
find a leprechaun
baseball team?

In the
Little League!